My Ever After Chronicles

By Carol Lynn Vengroff

Balboa Press books may be ordered through booksellers or by contacting:

Balboa Press
A Division of Hay House
1663 Liberty Drive
Bloomington, IN 47403
www.balboapress.com
1-(877) 407-4847

Because of the dynamic nature of the Internet, any web addresses or links contained in this book may have changed since publication and may no longer be valid. The views expressed in this work are solely those of the author and do not necessarily reflect the views of the publisher, and the publisher hereby disclaims any responsibility for them.

The author of this book does not dispense medical advice or prescribe the use of any technique as a form of treatment for physical, emotional, or medical problems without the advice of a physician, either directly or indirectly. The intent of the author is only to offer information of a general nature to help you in your quest for emotional and spiritual well-being. In the event you use any of the information in this book for yourself, which is your constitutional right, the author and the publisher assume no responsibility for your actions.

Any people depicted in stock imagery provided by Thinkstock are models, and such images are being used for illustrative purposes only. Certain stock imagery © Thinkstock.

ISBN: 978-1-4525-5977-3 (e)
ISBN: 978-1-4525-5976-6 (sc)
Library of Congress Control Number: 2012918059

Printed in the United States of America

Balboa Press rev. date: 11/05/2012

Dedicated with love and appreciation

to my mother and my father.

Dear Reader,

It is my sincere hope
that my writing brings you
Peace of mind,
Spiritual enlightenment,
Joy of heart,
Illumination to your soul and
Strikes a chord that resonates within,
Reminding you of your home in . . .
The Ever After.

Love and Light,
Carol

Acknowledgements:

My heartfelt and deepest gratitude:

to my husband Harvey,
son Travis and daughter Kristy
for always believing in me,

to my sisters Christine, Kathleen,
Lucille and BJ for cheering me on,

to my dear friends Kelly and Tony
for guiding me along my way,

and
to my teacher Carolyn for
validating my experience.

If you have wondered what happens after we die,
or where we come from before we are born . . .
If you have lost a loved one,
or have a life-threatening illness . . .
If you are going through heart wrenching times . . .
READ ON.

Contents

This is a true story.
It is my story.

Preface

Heaven

Many "experts" say that your religious beliefs, your expectations and your cultural influences shape your experience of Heaven.

As a twelve year old, my childhood would be changed forever, because that is when I personally had a near-death experience.

As a child, I believed that Heaven was a glowing city in the clouds, with pearly white gates, streets paved in gold. Angels in flowing gowns would be sitting on big puffy clouds playing harps and singing celestial songs. God would be seated on a golden throne, white hair, long beard and a white toga. He would be all aglow with Jesus standing by, dressed in white too. Only his hair would be long and light brown and he would have a golden staff and lambs by his feet.

Was I ever in for a surprise!

If what the experts say were true, I should have experienced my childhood vision of Heaven when I died. Instead, my Heaven was light-years from my religious beliefs, child-like expectations and cultural influences. The Heaven I experienced had never been mentioned in my world, back in the early 1960s. I was in uncharted territory!

There are no diplomas or degrees given out in Heaven. There really is no way of *proving* it exists, but it does.

I was there!

The Question

A group of close friends and I had taken one of our older girlfriends out to lunch for her milestone birthday. We were sitting around the restaurant table and catching up with each other's lives, when out of nowhere the birthday girl asked aloud: "I wonder what heaven is like?" Chatter in the room abruptly halted. This was a first. We weren't sure we heard correctly. Normally we keep our conversations pretty much down to earth and just chat about. . . girl stuff. Then she stood up and said: "I'm serious. . . what do you all think heaven is like"?

Being that our guest of honor was clearly not giving up on this topic, we looked at each other and decided to give it a try. It was really interesting going around the table and listening to all the theories, ideas and beliefs. One by one each guest attempted to answer this age-old question. As my turn got closer, my heart beat faster and I was overcome with mixed feelings. Part of me wanted get up and run, or at best become invisible, and another part of me wanted to stand on my chair and shout out:

"I KNOW! I HAVE THE ANSWER!!!"

These were my good friends and I didn't know if I should "go for it" and tell them my story and risk them never taking me seriously again, or play it safe and give a generic reply. I wasn't even sure if they really wanted an answer. When my turn finally did come and I went to speak, nothing came out of my mouth. I felt another wave of panic. I had lost my voice.

I wanted to share with everyone, but I just couldn't untangle all the words. Fear strangled my voice, clouded my mind, and silenced my heart. Her question triggered something deep within me, jump-starting a long-lost memory and a flood of unexpected emotions. What was going on with me? I took a deep breath, than another, then decided to just lighten up and confess.

I was one of *those* people who had had a near-death experience and, though mine was very similar to many, it was also very unique. I answered the question of the day as best I could, and though the birthday girl was happy with what I had to say, the conversations that my answer generated were surprising to me. Some expressed doubt, some shared their own spiritual encounters, others said they really appreciated what I had to say, and some had even more questions for me.

That day was supposed to be about my friend's birthday, and it was, but it also was a milestone day for me. It was the first time I had talked with a group of girlfriends about "heaven". I had finally taken a step onto a path that was to be the beginning of a personal journey. This journey would eventually lead to writing this account of my amazing experience. This is my attempt to put into words and chronicle my near-death experience, my first hand encounter of Life Before We Arrive Here, Life After Death, The Afterlife, Eternity, Bliss, The Other Side, Nirvana, Everlasting Life, Paradise, The Ever After…
Heaven.

Where Do I Begin?

The year was 1963. I was twelve years old. My father was a pilot in the U.S. Air Force and he was stationed at Evreux Air Base outside of Paris, France. His tour was to last three years, and our family was lucky enough to join him and live off base in a three-hundred-year-old chateau on a gentleman's farm.

I am the oldest girl of six children. With two older brothers and three younger sisters, we were quite a brood. As diverse as we all were, we had one thing in common; a love of travel. We decided as a family to spend our Christmas vacation that year exploring Italy.

We returned from our Christmas holiday, arriving home in the middle of the night, exhausted from a nonstop eighteen-hour drive. As fate would have it, we missed an ice storm, but ran right into one of the coldest nights in France's recorded history. There was no heat, no running water, and no electricity in our house because our furnace had run out of coal; all the water pipes had frozen, and power lines were down.

Chilled to the bone, we went to our frigid beds with our hats and coats on, and wool mufflers wrapped around our necks. But this wasn't enough to shield me from the icy air. I couldn't get warm. As I lay shivering in my bed, an unexpected sensation started to take over my body.

First my hands and feet lost feeling, and then my arms and legs went completely numb. I remember the strange feeling of fading away, each part of me slowly succumbing to the freezing cold.

I felt myself drift off . . . first into an abyss of inky darkness, and then into the light.

Into the Light and Gravity Free

I felt complete.
I felt safe.
I felt loved!

At first I thought I was dreaming. I sensed that I was traveling through a void, a chasm, deep space. As I was moving, I experienced each detail of my life up to that instant, as if for the very first time. I had total recall from the moment I was born to that actual night.

I experienced a crystal-clear, staggeringly detailed review of everything I had ever felt, seen, touched, smelled, tasted, heard, sensed, and done. What astounded me was that, simultaneously, I also experienced my life review from the vantage point of everyone and everything with which I had ever come into contact. I observed how every single thing I had ever done, connected with, and had an effect on everyone and everything. I witnessed not only how my actions and deeds, but also how my thoughts and feelings had a universal ripple effect! I was astonished!

As I was re-living my *human* life, it occurred to me that my actions were not being assessed by anyone but me. I was not being judged by a higher power. *I* was the one who was my own judge and jury.

At the same time, I also saw that at every moment of my life, God was and had always been with me. God was a vigilant parent, keeping watch over me. I also understood how God was in everything and united us all!

I was filled with overwhelming joy. I had the sense that I was somewhere that I had been before; somewhere peaceful, somewhere wonderful, like a familiar pathway to my home, like a long-lost friend. As memories kept flooding my being, I traveled onward through time and space.

The farther I traveled, the less gravity had a hold on me, until finally I was gravity-free. I was totally body-free!

In the distance I could see a light, and the light became pixilated, almost playful, as I was drawn into it.

Suddenly, I came to a dead stop. I had arrived. I had arrived at a place that defied description in human terms. I had returned to a consciousness of timeless existence, of perfect vibration, resonation, light, illumination, joy and love. There were no words in our human language that even came remotely close to being able to describe the dimension I had entered.

I was enveloped by illumination, a radiant light like nothing I had ever seen or experienced. It was like being inside of a pulsating, dazzling, brilliant, glowing cloud and at the same time I was gleaming from within.

I had shed the human form that I had taken on to house myself and to contain my soul while I was on earth. My spirit and soul were still me. I was still the same essence but now I had the ability to understand the experience of expansiveness and, I would be able to assimilate all the information that being a free spirit entailed.

This was a place without time. Hours, minutes, seconds, night, day, months, years, centuries, eons did not exist. Yet, there was an order, a system to everything taking place.

There was no temperature, no hot nor cold, no weather, no atmosphere, yet I was perfectly comfortable.

I was aware that I was not alone and was able to communicate in an all-encompassing language without talking, without speech or words. We were interconnecting on levels and dimensions that were not possible as human beings.

There was sound, but the sounds that surrounded me were nothing like I had ever heard before. The clarity, resonance, and tones were infinitely richer and clearer. Not only did each note take on a life of its own, but vibrated and resonated in perfect harmony and in frequencies that I knew to be flawless and sacred. These sounds were encoded and were energetically connected to creation. The sounds were layered with what seemed like voices, instruments and waves of frequencies, coming together to create thrilling, beautiful music.

Even my sense of smell was different. I absorbed the most wonderful fragrances. The rich, pure scents were both mesmerizing and a welcome addition to all that I was encountering. Even fragrance had transformational abilities!

All my senses were indescribably amplified and heightened in a way I had never experienced on earth. I felt real. I felt more alive, more than I could ever remember.

This place resonated in perfect vibration, and I was in perfect harmony within it.

I was home!

My Greeters

Then from out of nowhere, a *soul* came to greet me. It was my mother's father, and he was there to welcome me. My grandfather had passed away years before I was born. I have no idea how I knew he was my grandfather, yet I knew it was him. It was his tender spirit that was there to welcome me. We both were overjoyed to be together. Although, on a human level we had never met, I actually remembered having missed him. We carried on a loving conversation without words.

I was aware of multi-dimensional experiences and a depth of knowledge that my twelve-year-old child could not have begun to imagine in life.

I was completely an entity unto myself, and there were many others who were as unique as I was. It was like being in a dense mist and sensing other people near me. Though I could not see them as we humans see, I recognized and was thankful for each and every one of them, as they welcomed me back. We had known each other before we'd gone to earth, and had always known that we would be united together again, upon our return.

There were hundreds, thousands, countless numbers of beings, spirits, and souls of all kinds: family members, ancestors, friends, teachers, students, angels, archangels, seraphims, prophets, wise entities, divine beings, light bodies and enlightened masters.

We were all united; we were all conscious of a connecting bind and overwhelming link of pure joy, realized peace, expanding, illuminating light and resonating, escalating, transcending love!

There were no structures or buildings, but I had an impression that I was entering an important chamber-like hall that resembled a courtroom. The air was somber. Sitting to the left behind a long, towering judge's dais, were a tribunal of Light Beings who were different from all the other beings that I had encountered so far.
They were "Keepers of Knowledge".
They *were* Knowledge!

We conversed for a long time. I asked them questions I could not have thought of as the child I had been, and they answered each one. I remember thinking that their responses were in realms and dimensions that I could never have even begun to comprehend on earth.

I laughed and said, "Now I understand why this place can't be explained." They replied: "There are no words, within the realm of the human experience, which are able to describe most of these answers ."

As a child, I'd been taught to call that place "heaven," but now that name seemed totally inadequate.
I realized then, and now, that
              it is not a place at all,
                         it is a state of being. . .
a milieu that our soul, our spirit and our essence inhabit before we are born, and after we die.

As I was contemplating all that was transpiring, I felt a shift occur from within, and I was aware of a new aspect of this experience starting to unfold. I was in awe as I felt my heart starting to open and expand, and overflow with love. Something wonderful was happening. I was keenly aware that I wasn't just me anymore. I was part of a love-bond without boundaries, in a perfect relationship that transcended time and form. I felt love beyond imagination.

It was the love of Christ!

It was Christ!

He came to me and I was overcome with joy and happiness. My heart was eternally grateful to be reunited with Him.

The Christ I experienced there was nothing like the Christ I was taught about here on earth.

Though He was in spirit there, I remembered Him as a human being.

I remembered him as a humble, brilliant, straightforward, uncomplicated, unadorned, easily approachable man.

I remembered him having a heart so saturated in love that there was no need for forgiveness in it.

He was incapable of feeling harm or hate towards anything or anyone.

He was so pure that he resonated at an unseen frequency that actually healed and uplifted many who just came into his path.

He was wise beyond comprehension.

He was truth! Perfect knowledge!

His energy was so sacred and high that he illuminated from within. Though most could not see his light, they sensed it on many levels.

When he spoke, he measured his words carefully and his Aramaic dialect had power. Each Aramaic word resonated and vibrated and took on a life of its own. Each word he spoke illuminated with a *light* of its own!

When he prayed he connected directly to God!

When he meditated, he recharged his soul.

I remembered how he looked. . . with a lean body, dark shoulder length hair, and eyes that looked right through you to your very soul!

He had a disarming smile.

His voice was captivating and his laugh infectious. He actually had a sense of humor.

His hands were both gentle and powerful and were just as capable of building a chair or throwing a fish net, as they were of healing a broken body or bestowing a blessing.

He was beautiful.

He was charismatic.

I remembered everything about Him!

I was in bliss just being near him.

I remembered how much I had missed him.

I never wanted to leave His side again.

GOD Realization

J ust when I thought that my heart, soul, and essence had reached the saturation point of rapture and that I wanted to be in that moment forever,
an even higher,
    absolutely perfect,
        all-encompassing
            and rapidly expanding wave
                swept over me.

This sensation soared through me, through my heart, and it completely united all of us there, together as one. It was. . . it is. . . the perfect vibration, exhilarating joy, pure truth, radiating light, and overwhelming love; the unrestrained, constantly expanding, experience of God!

I was aware that this was what it was like to realize God, Essence, Spirit, Life-force, The All-powerful All-knowing, Jehovah, Creator of the Universe, *I Am*!

So this was what it was like to realize God; the thread, the light, the love, the vibration that runs through us, illuminates us and connects all.

God is perfect vibration, light, every number, and pure, overwhelming, amazing, spectacular love in every form, sense and possibility.

So this was what it was like to be part of the sacred codes and resonation that birth creativity and unite and bond all.

God frequency is so perfect, so luminescent, so delicately calibrated and resonates at such a high and perfect vibration that there is only room for pure JOY.

So this was what it was like to feel how judgment does not exist for God!

God's truth and love are so saturating and dense that evil cannot exist within that truth and love. God is all knowing. God has always been and will always be.

So this was God realization!!!

My very essence was totally, wholly and absolutely in peace. I had dissolved into the I AM!

Knowledge Beyond
Comprehension

The work is this:
There is nothing to do,
Just be the light that you are!

I was given the answers to every question
and I understood everything there is to understand.

The following is my very humble attempt
to put into words,
the knowledge I obtained from the
Tribunal of Light Beings:

Message:

There is a message, and the message is so simple that it
can be summed up within these words:
Do not Harm.
Harm nothing with hate.
Love one another!

Forgiveness:

I had an epiphany of how this one word, forgiveness,
holds within, a power so strong that it can heal the world,

dissolve disease and bring mankind to a true and enlightened existence. The key to allowing our light to illuminate and to radiate is by clearing our hearts of any and all forgiveness issues.

Light:

I saw how light is energy unto itself, with frequencies that originated in the divinity and sacredness of God. I remembered that the light was always with us and although we may have had human bodies, we had within. . . light bodies!

I realized that we sometimes forgot who we were because we got caught up in the drama of being human.

Some of us covered over our light by becoming distracted with material possessions.

Some believed stories that kept us from truth or made excuses for how we showed up in life.

Some were seduced by carnal experiences.

Some, sidetracked by entities that depleted our energy.

Some of us became overwhelmed and overloaded with emotions and feelings and disease.

I was reminded that we originated as spirit-filled light beings and that we ultimately would return to our spirit-filled light beings.

Knowledge:

There was so much more than what I could comprehend in human terms. The knowledge that I obtained there was light years beyond human understanding and experience. And although I was able to assimilate it all there, I am not able to remember all of it here.

Love:

The most powerful force in the universe is love. As the sacred emotion of God, love transcends all. It is our true state of being. There is only love.

Prayer:

I understood that prayers from the heart ride vibration frequencies to God. I witnessed how a thought became an intent, how the intent became a word, how the word became a prayer, and how the prayer became a manifestation.

Vibration:

Pure, crystal-clear, resonating frequencies pulsated through all, connecting everyone, everything and every universe to God. I saw divine frequencies, vibrating and connecting micro cosmos creations to macro cosmos creations.

Celestial music:

The music I experienced there was sacred, moving and almost magical in that it also took on a life and energy of its own, connecting with me, and becoming a part of me. It was performed, or I should say resonated in frequencies that are beyond the human experience. In hearing wind chimes, tuning forks, sacred bowls, symphonies, melodies that touch my heart, harmonies that bring me to tears, compositions and songs that touch my soul, the Solfeggio frequencies, ancient chants, bird, whale and dolphin calls, I am reminded of the music I encountered there.

Information:

When I was in that endlessly expanding state, I realized that the information I was receiving transcended all reason and boundaries.   I understood that anything was possible and I realized that it was from that state of heart we agreed, to come back to earth, and to give life a try. Sometimes over and over again. Some of us came as teachers and some as students. They came not in a judgmental way, but just in a playful and pre-arranged agreement way. Some of us came back for a very specific reason and to master a particular life lesson. Some of us returned as light beings or light workers, and had within, a radiance that would be a beacon for others.

Sacred geometry:

All the patterns of creation are contained within sacred geometry and carry within them codes that hold the keys to knowledge beyond our imagination. I believe that everything in the universe has its roots based in this. I saw how numbers were woven into the fabric of everything that exists. I saw how a myriad of numbers had sacred significance. The concept that music and number systems are perfect universal language was firmly planted in my soul.

The evidence showed up everywhere:

Universal Harmonic Series at 144Hz,
The Music of Transformation at 432Hz,
The Golden Ratio 108,
Fibonacci Sequence,
Phi 1.918...
Harmonic Ratios
Flower of Life,
Music of the Spheres

are but a fraction of samples.

I *understood that meditation and prayer created the*
space wherein all was possible.

I *was illuminated throughout attaining the Divine,*
realizing God!

B*y just being the light that we are, we are*
accomplishing our mission.

My Return

I felt like I had been there for a lifetime but it must have been for only a few moments. Then I was somehow made to understand that I could not stay. They said I had to go back and complete my life. Then I heard a voice say to me that I had an assignment to complete on earth. At that very moment a specific mission was simultaneously dictated to me and planted in my heart. I was told that after my mission back on earth was complete, I would be able to return. But for now, I had to leave.

The next thing I remember was wondering how they were going to condense and fit my cosmos-expanded light-being of joy, love, and contentment, that was now me, back into that tiny, microscopic speck of a particle that was my twelve-year-old human body, lying in a bed somewhere

way . . . way . . . way . . .
down on that planet, light years and lifetimes away.

In what seemed like an instant, I was catapulted, sucked and drawn back into my body, and pulled in by an overpowering magnetic and gravitational force.

Suddenly, I felt weighed down with such heaviness that I was positive it would suffocate and paralyze me. My spirit, my essence, and my physical body were united once again. I was back in me, back in my bed, back in France, back in the year 1963.

The journey back was excruciating. I hurt all over. I was confused and in shock. How long had I been gone? What had I just experienced?

Gravity was so heavy that I was sure I wouldn't be able to move at all from its weight. I felt as if I wouldn't be able to take a breath, but I did.

I took one breath, and then another. I started to move one icy finger at a time, then my toes, and then my limbs. My eyes popped open. It was still dark and I was freezing cold.

I woke up our sleeping household, half-hysterical, trying to explain what had just happened to me. My parents were cold, exhausted, and cranky from our long drive home from Italy. They were not thrilled to have their sleep disturbed, and even less so to be woken up in the pre-dawn hours by a confused child claiming to have just died!

My mother dismissed what I was so eager to explain as a dream. My siblings had no idea what I was talking about, and my father ordered me to go back to bed, saying, "We will discuss this further in the morning".

In a little red diary that I kept at that time, I hand-wrote a cryptic note to myself. On the page dated January 6, 1963, my entry read: "I woke up at 3:00 a.m." Only I would understand what that sentence meant.

When morning arrived, my parents were still upset. They kept telling me it was a dream and that I had an overactive imagination. When I insisted that I had been sent back here with information to share, a mission to complete, they became very concerned. When I explained what this was, it was understandably more than they were willing to tolerate.

Not knowing what to do with me, they had me meet with our church chaplain, who was also our close family friend. I was positive that he would be elated with my news. I felt that if anyone would understand and embrace my experience and my mission, he would. I was completely stunned and taken aback when he said, "If you ever repeat this nonsense to anyone, I will strongly urge your parents to have you put away".

I was devastated. My spirit, heart, and world were shattered. No adult believed me and even worse, they thought that I'd lost my mind. I was ordered to stop talking about it.

I devised a plan. If I couldn't talk about it, then I would write about it. So I penciled a letter to myself, carefully chronicling the information I was given, in what I now know was my near-death experience. After I was satisfied that I had included everything I could remember, I took the paper, folded it into a compact package, and wrapped it in a protective tinfoil casing. Then I placed my precious parcel in a hidden nook in a stone wall that surrounded our property at my house in France.

I drew a secret map in the back of my diary showing the exact location of my hiding place in the wall. I promised myself that one day I would come back, retrieve the letter, share the information and complete my mission. I was positive that as an adult, my story would finally be believed.

I was sent back from the Ever After with information to share. I was sent back here with a mission to complete, an agenda to carry out, but it would have to wait. I would have to wait, and wait I did.

Remembering

As the years passed by, the memory of my experience faded away. I was busy with school, then college, my career, marriage and family. I got caught up with life. Though I tucked my near-death experience deep within, I always felt a very strong connection with God. My life was blessed and divinely guided and I was grateful.

It wasn't until I turned forty that I started to get flashbacks of my childhood and that night. I sensed that I was supposed to remember something but I couldn't quite remember what it was. Like pieces of a puzzle, all the parts of my life were slowly starting to fit together. Enlightened insight and cryptic dreams started to show up. I questioned the religious beliefs that I grew up with. The more my world, heart and mind started to open up and expand, the more I noticed how everything in my life was starting to connect. There are no coincidences.

At fifty years old, I started to recall even more of my childhood experiences and more details about that pre-dawn morning in 1963. With the help and collective memories of my sisters, I was able to start to put together even more pieces of my vague puzzle. We started to fill in the blanks. I started in earnest to journal and write my thoughts, feelings and ideas down. I painted in my studio while listening to music that touched my soul. I sailed, I walked the beach, I planted a garden. At night I searched the heavens, the internet and manuscripts for answers which lead me to more questions.

Finally at Sixty, I knew that I had to re-examine my near-death experience. Though I was seeing a clear picture appear, a lot of pieces to my puzzle were still missing. I was positive there was something important I needed to remember. I just wasn't sure what it was.

Divine Guidance

I prayed for guidance and direction, and I was led to find a course offered online through Atlantic University, called "Near-Death Experience Survivors: Finding Your Mission". Carolyn Matthews created it and she was the instructor. It was as if the universe put this module out there just for me. The timing was perfect.

I decided to take action and I enrolled. I just made the deadline and was the last student accepted into the class. With the encouragement of my family, I jumped feet first into this exciting endeavor.

The course was magical.

Carolyn gave us soul-searching assignments. Each week we had to turn in themed papers. She set up an online participants' website so that we had a forum to share experiences and support each other.

We were asked to keep a journal of our assignments, observations and thoughts. I jotted down every word, impression, and idea as they showed up.

We recorded our dreams along with our interpretations. Some of mine were so real that I was astounded. The meanings and messages they revealed were startling.

We were encouraged to find a quiet place for meditating without interruption.

I started to feel a shift in my energy, spirit, and self. It was as if the assignments unlocked a portal to my soul.

Once the door was open, memories, information, and visions from my near-death experience started to come flooding back. I was able to see how all the pieces of my life's puzzle were coming together. I was able to define exactly what my earthly creative talent was and I saw a glimpse of how and where I was going to use it. The only missing piece was still hiding in my heart. Ironically, the one part of my near-death experience that I couldn't recall or more likely just was not ready to face, was the mission I was sent back to carry out. I wasn't concerned because I knew that in time, when I was ready, I would remember it again.

Carolyn's support and encouragement were energizing. With her guidance I was able to help myself to not only see the light but to also find my voice. But the most important part of this whole process was that *finally*, someone believed in me, believed that I really had a near-death experience and actually wanted to hear what I had to say.

FINALLY, I felt validated!

Paris in the Springtime

In the spring of 2011, I decided to make a pilgrimage back to my old house in France to search for the letter I had written about my experience and more importantly, my mission, nearly fifty years before.

With my little red diary in hand, and a dear friend by my side, we followed the secret map's directions to the exact location where I had hidden it.

My letter had long since disintegrated, but the tinfoil I had wrapped it in was there! The visit back was nothing short of amazing. Just being there unlocked even more memories. Though I went looking for physical proof, I had already received answers to most of my questions. The answers had always been within me.

The more I quieted my mind and opened my heart, the more I connected to God.

The more I connected to God, the easier it became to remember and to relive my experience of life in the Ever After.

The only missing piece was recalling my mission. I believed that I was supposed to have delivered a very specific message. This was the main reason why I was sent back to earth.

The message was still secure within my heart, right behind a thin veil and almost within my grasp. I was on the cusp of remembering what it was.

Finally, almost half a century later, and when I had nearly completed this manuscript; I had an extraordinary moment of enlightenment. While in a very deep meditative state, I was able to the return to that moment in time; my near-death experience. It was then that I heard a crystal-clear voice say to me:

"Your assignment is this:
Go to the Pope and give him this message:
Melt down your golden altars and feed your people!"

My mission may have appeared to be a very simple sentence, but if carried out; its directive could have enormous ramifications.

Then it hit me like a lightning bolt and it became obvious why it took me forever to remember it. It wasn't so much that I couldn't remember, it was more likely that the twelve-year-old child in me did not want to remember. Finally, I was in a place in my life where it was safe to remember my long lost mission from heaven.

Mission

Not only was I then in a place in my life where I felt it was safe to remember, but I was also in a place in my life where I could actually carry out this assignment.

There are no coincidences, and just as soon as I recalled my mission, the opportunity for me to set it into motion presented itself.

As it turned out, my best friend occasionally hosted a delegate from the Vatican at her home. He wore many hats within the Roman Catholic Church, one being an ambassador for the Pope.

She set up a meeting between the two of us. At our meeting, I told him my story and I asked him what I should do about delivering the message. He asked if I was comfortable sharing my mission with him. After a few moments, I decided I would. I was not sure if the skies would open and I would get struck down by lightening, or if he would be so offended that he would turn his back on me and simply leave the room.

My message had fifty years to ferment while it was hidden inside my heart. It held a lifetime of fears and disillusions.

So, it was with great trepidation that I took a deep breath, looked him straight in the eye, then slowly and carefully recited the mission I had been given to deliver to the Pope from the Ever After.

This was it. . . I finally got it out! I was FREE. . .or so I thought.

There was a moment of hesitation. Then, with a slight smile making its way across his face and into his eyes, he said it would not be necessary to bring my message to the Pope. After another long moment he said: "We are very aware of this sentiment. We hear it all the time. This is not a new idea."

He went on to explain why the Catholic Church had not acted on this directive, and politely explained that it would never, in all probability, act on it, but appreciated what I was saying. He understood how important this moment was for me and he respected that.

He also said if I should choose to include this discussion in my writing, that he felt the Catholic Church would have no problem with it.

Of course I now realize that the message of: *"Melt down your golden altars and feed your people"* is widely understood, and the sentiment is shared by many in our troubled world.

I was finalizing the last draft for this book and had completed it up to this point and I was content with my mission accomplished story ending. I really wanted to leave it as is, to cross "My Mission" off my bucket list and to call it a day. I had delivered my message, maybe not to the actual Pope, but to his emissary.

But... my heart is telling me something different. I am not finished. My mission is not complete. I have, at this very moment, decided that I will see my mission from God through to the end. I have no idea how or when it will happen yet, but I know it will. This feels right. This is right.

I will use my creative talents and all that I have learned from the ever after and all my prayer and meditative insight to complete my mission and have my audience with the Pope. I will sit eye to eye, heart to heart and spirit to spirit with the Pontiff, and finally deliver these powerful *nine** words: ("Melt down your golden altars and feed your people") that were to be delivered directly from God, through me, to him. My soul knows that he will be expecting me.

*nine:

The spiritual value of the number Nine is the very pinnacle of vibrational frequencies. Nine represents attainment, satisfaction, accomplishment, successful achievement and influence. It deals with intellectual power, inventiveness, influence over situations and things. It begs us to recognize our own internal power, and implores us to extend these abilities out into the world to make a positive, influential difference.

Lessons

Lessons
Messages from the Ever After

Answers
The message is simple; looking back it will all make sense.

Who we are
Before we arrived, we chose the vessel that would house our soul, spirit, energy and light. We chose the circumstances and we set the stage. We chose the experience.

Our personal mission
Each and every one of us is here for a reason. Each of us has a gift to share, a creative talent, a contribution to make, a chance to raise the vibration of each other and our planet.

Perfect plan
It is all perfect, every single part of our life. . . every single incident, seeming coincidence, event, encounter and decision. Every single moment is part of a perfect plan, part of our journey and we get all our answers in the end.

Choice
Along our journey we make choices. We get to decide which path to choose, which door to open and which step to take. It is not what happens to us that matters, but how we

interpret and embrace each and every thing that comes into our life. When one door closes, another door opens.

Human experience
We are spirit, temporarily housed in a physical form, having a human experience in a material world. In this form and experience we have parameters and definitive boundaries. Time and form are our temporary limitations. Gravity keeps us grounded.

Family
We travel in packs and we know each other from heaven, and we will be there together again when we leave this earth.

Possibilities
When we see the possibilities in every aspect of our life, we connect with God. When we see possibilities, our hearts open and pathways for miracles and transformation to occur, emerge.

Messages
When one door is firmly shut or slammed in our face, perhaps it is a STRONG message being sent to us! Be grateful and realize that now we know what we are NOT supposed to do!

Connect to God
Prayer, meditation and breath and are ways to connect to God. Music, art, nature and laughter are others.

The Answer

What is Heaven like? I know what it's like. It was nothing like I thought it would be as a child. It is incredibly, astoundingly and mind-blowing amazing! I know that my spirit and soul never die, and so, I am not afraid of my physical death. I just borrowed this body, this vessel, to temporarily house my essence while I am visiting earth and having a human experience. I know exactly where I came from before this life. I know precisely where I am going after this life. And there is everything to look forward to, because in the end,

the end . . .

is just . . .

the beginning!

Notes:

Questions:

Epiphanies: